Moody Currier

Early Poems

Moody Currier

Early Poems

ISBN/EAN: 9783744711067

Printed in Europe, USA, Canada, Australia, Japan

Cover: Foto ©Thomas Meinert / pixelio.de

More available books at **www.hansebooks.com**

EARLY POEMS

BY

MOODY CURRIER.

MANCHESTER, N. H.:
PUBLISHED BY JOHN B. CLARKE.
1881.

PUBLISHER'S NOTICE.

This volume is a reprint of one published last year by its author for private circulation among his personal friends. The poems it contains were written by him as a recreation during his leisure hours, and were first published without any purpose of making them public property ; but since that time there has come to us an urgent and somewhat extensive demand for copies from the general public, which has induced us to urge upon Mr. Currier the propriety of permitting us to publish, on our own account, a new edition for general circulation. To this he has consented, and we now offer the work to the public.

JOHN B. CLARKE.

MANCHESTER, N. H., May, 1881.

CONTENTS.

	PAGE
STANZAS	5
THE ROSEMARY	7
CAMILLA'S STAR	9
THE PAST	11
A REMEMBERED FRIEND	15
THE COQUETTE	17
FROM THE GERMAN	21
BUNKER HILL	23
STANZAS	27
A PASTORAL	29
THE ADIEU	32
LONELY MUSINGS	34
TELL HIM I'LL WAKE AGAIN	36
THE DAY OF BATTLE	38
NATURE A PROOF OF GOD'S EXISTENCE	42
WRITTEN ON ONE OF THE WESTERN MOUNDS	44
THE MIND UNCHANGEABLE	47
MIND FEEDS ON THOUGHT	49
THE INDIAN	52
SCENES FROM A DREAM	54
O'ER EGYPT'S PLAINS	58
WHY PLUCK THE FLOWERS?	60
THE WANDERER	62
THE MIND IS ETERNAL	68
A VISIT TO WASHINGTON	70
HYMN FOR THE NEW YEAR	73
THERE IS A WREATH	75
DREAMING	77

CONTENTS.

What I've Seen	79
The Progress of Society	81
To Delia	86
We See no Hostile Blade	88
Mignon	91
The Wanderer's Lot	93
New Year's Address	96
Greece	105
The Mountain Shepherd's Song	107
Spring	109
Hope. — To Mary	111
The Graveyard	113
An Imitation of Mignon	116
If I were a Child	119
The Mountain Shepherd	122
An Evening Sketch	125
The Ghost Student	131
They Call me Infidel	137
Man and Woman	141
Not Glory's Plume	146
Lines Written in a Young Lady's Album at School	148
On Recovering from Sickness	150
On the Death of a Young Lady	152
The One who is far away	154
A Dream	156
Written in an Album	158
Adam Lays the Blame on Eve	160
All Things Change	162
Remembered Joys	164
The Orphans	165
The Poet's Fame	168
Over the River	170
October	172
Morn	174
Where was God?	175
The Indians	179

STANZAS.

A HEBREW MELODY.

Soft winds still blow o'er Jordan's stream,
　And curl its restless flood,
As when along its banks of green
　The sons of Judah trod.

The stars look down as fair and bright,
　On hill and plain and stream,
As when the Prophet watched at night
　Their silver shining beam.

On Carmel's distant waving fields
  Still creeps the clustering vine;
And still the rose of Sharon yields
  Its fragrant sweets divine.

Though winds are soft and stars are bright,
  O'er distant fields and flood,
As when the beams of sacred light
  Shone round the Ark of God;

No more is heard the Levite's song,
  No more the Prophet's dream;
No more the choral virgin throng
  On Zion's hill is seen.

The Hebrew maids in Gentile lands
  Now seek an exile's home;
And where their fathers' grave-stones stand,
  The sons of Hagar roam.

THE ROSEMARY.*

There is a flower that never dies;

   Its beauties ever bloom;

Among the dead its petals rise,

   And cling around the tomb.

When winter's storms are cold and drear,

   And fierce the tempests rave,

Its brightest flowerets then appear,

   And smile upon the grave.

* The rosemary is said to bloom in winter, and is planted around graves and tombs by mourning friends, as an emblem of that love and friendship which lives even in death.

Come, sweetest flower, a wreath I'll twine,
    To friendship's sacred name;
A brighter, holier branch than thine,
    Not friendship's self can claim.

Like youthful love, thy summer bower
    A living fragrance brings;
Like friendship's tear, thy wintry flower
    'Mid cheerless tempests springs.

" Come, fun'ral flower," I'll plant thy root
    Beneath the cypress shade;
And let thy lowly blossoms shoot
    Where man's last home is made.

And when, sweet flower, that home is mine,
    A living perfume shed;
And kindly o'er the lonely shrine
    Thy softest tendrils spread.

CAMILLA'S STAR.

Say, bright twinkling orb of light,
Trembling on the verge of night,
As you pass your earthly round,
If on earth a name you've found,
Dearer than the one you bear,
Dearer than Camilla's star?

Though you shine with clearer light,
Fairest of the train of night,
Though are lost beneath your blaze
Many a feebler planet's rays,—

Brighter honors you may claim,
Whilst you wear Camilla's name.

When at summer's eve you rise,
Chasing darkness from the skies,
Then I'll watch thee, and regret
When thy circling course is set;
Set or rise, I'll sing thy fame,
Whilst thou bear'st Camilla's name.

Now perhaps she looks on thee,
Without a thought or care for me;
Forming, as thy courses move,
Dearer objects for her love;
Objects who will ne'er declare
Love for thee, Camilla's star.

THE PAST.

Hope may shine with beamy light,
   Down the vale of fancied fears,
And gild the curtained folds of night
   That hang o'er future years,—
But Doubt intrudes with ruffian hand,
And tears away our fairy-land;
And Reason sees but forms of air
Float swift o'er scenes of coming care.

Joy is ne'er a present boon,
   Placed within our mortal grasp,

But lies amidst the future's gloom,
    Or lingers in the *past*.
Our restless passions never rest;
A thousand thoughts distract the breast;
And all we feel or love below
Alternate ebb, alternate flow.

Scenes of former days are bright;
    Time dispels the shades of woe;
There only pleasures live in light,
    And loveliest prospects glow.
On mem'ry's page life's rugged scenes
Like phantoms flit; their trembling beams
Have lost their hostile guise; they move
Amidst the lingering forms we love.

Days of youth! I see them rise,
    Smiling in the distant past; —

The cloudless morn, the rainbow skies,
    In deathless beauty last.
In fields I loved, I see but flowers;
No thorns I find among the bowers;
An angel's hand hath sure been there,
And nothing left but bright and fair.

Foes, that snatched with hostile hands
    Hope's soft cheering gifts away,
Transformed, like fabled fairy bands,
    Now stand in bright array;—
And now are hid in flowery crowns
The angry look, the threat'ning frowns,
Whilst every form, with beauty's bloom,
Now smiles amidst the distant gloom.

Love, that springs in infant breasts,
    Pure as Eden's purest flame,

THE PAST.

Behind the curtains of the past,

Seems still a nymph of heavenly name.

The artless lip, the rosy cheek,

In kindly accents seem to speak,

As oft the muse with kindling haste

And " wing of fire " explores the past.

A REMEMBERED FRIEND.

"I will leave off as I begun."— D. WEBSTER.

They say she is wrinkled and old,
    That the tint of the rose-bud is gone;
That her smile is unmeaning and cold,
    And her countenance sad and forlorn;—
But still to my fancy she seems
    Like a beautiful blossom of spring;
And, amid the delusion of dreams,
    Her smiles to my memory cling.

Her step seems as light to my view,
  As when in her childhood she moved;
And the blush on her cheek is as new
  And as fresh as the one that I loved;—
But they say she is wrinkled and old,
  That the tint of the rose-bud is gone;
That her smile is unmeaning and cold,
  And her countenance sad and forlorn.

THE COQUETTE.

A SONG.

I saw a flower, — 'twas bright and fair,
    And beauteous as the morn;
Its petals fluttered in the air
    That played around its form.

Though many a flower around it grew,
    As envious of its charms,
And decked with blossoms ever new,
    Upreared their varied forms, —

Yet none was found so bright and fair,
    Of all the flowery race;
Nor could their gaudy tints compare
    With simple, artless grace.

The rose-bud blushed beneath the gaze
    Of every ravished eye,
And smiled to hear the lavish praise
    Of every passer-by.

The zephyr stole the balmy sweet,
    That floated round its head;
Whilst from the sunbeam's ardent heat,
    Its dewy honors fled.

The insect drank the nectar tear,
    That trembled in the morn;
And oft, in wanton riot here,
    Despoiled its varied form.

Thus ev'ry hand was stretched to claim
   This lovely vernal gem;
Till, torn and pale, it soon became
   A withered, wilted stem.

But many a flower around it grew,
   Unnoticed and forlorn,
Whose brightest blossoms still were new,
   When all its own were gone.

And on the rose-bud's rifled charms,
   Not e'en a look was cast;
But lone and drear, its faded form
   Was pelted by the blast.

'Tis thus I've seen a blooming fair,
   By all around caressed;
A thousand proffered hearts were there,
   And hope in ev'ry breast.

There now remains a cheerless one,
Of hope and joy bereft;
A heaving sigh, a smothered groan,
Oft swell the stricken breast.

While many a homely cheek retains
Its smile and flush of youth,
Nor feels the bitter pangs and pains
Of oft-neglected truth.

FROM THE GERMAN.

Close beside a rocky summit,
   Where a stilly brooklet flows,
'Neath a darkly spreading willow,
   Be my place of last repose;
In that vale of coolest shade,
Let this aching heart be laid.

Hath thy bosom's idol shunned thee,
   Once so beautiful and fair,
Though thy tears of bitter anguish
   Marked thy wasting, deep despair,—

Seek an end for all thy woes,
Where that stilly brooklet flows.

All my hopes of joy are vanished;
 All my prayers are turned to scorn;
Close beside that rocky summit,
 Let this wasted form be borne, —
In that vale, I'll seek repose,
Where that stilly brooklet flows.

BUNKER HILL.

A DREAM.

On Bunker's height methought I stood,
    And gazed o'er hill and plain:
Its brow was wet with patriot blood;
    Its sides were heaped with slain.

Before me rise, in dread array,
    A spectred warrior band;
In thickening files they crowd the way;
    In shadowy squadrons stand.

Nor cap nor plume their heads adorn,
    No soldier's coat they wear;
The garb of peace hangs round their form,
    And freedom's shield they bear.

As when they left the half-ploughed field,
    And weeping child and wife,
For freemen's rights their arms to wield,
    And freely gave their life, —

So still they move, a fearless band,
    Where once they bravely fought,
And, joyful still, watch o'er the land
    Their toil and blood have bought.

Here Warren stands, whose patriot arm
    Was raised for human right,
As when he drove the hireling swarm
    From Bunker's bloody height.

There Putnam rides through hurrying files,
    As when he pressed the foe,
And swift the flying bands assailed,
    Nor spared the dreadful blow.

"Ye shades of mighty men!" I said,
    "Who guard this hallowed shrine,
Wherein the bones and dust are laid
    Of men almost divine,

"Here heroes fell, here patriots bled;
    This spot is holy ground,
'The sepulchre of mighty dead,'
    With stainless glory crowned.

"Oh, watch the noblest, holiest dust
    That sleeps on 'glory's bed;'
Ye leave this soil, a sacred trust,
    The spot whereon ye bled."

Then rank and column swiftly passed,
   As light as lightest air;
Nor cannon's roar, nor musket's flash,
   Nor drum nor shout was there.

STANZAS.

"I would not wear the fairest flower"
    That e'er in Eden grew,
Although 't were plucked from angel's bower
    And wet with heavenly dew,
If e'er 't had shed its virgin bloom
    Around another's brow,
And yielded once its rich perfume,
    To passing friend or foe.

I would not wed the fairest maid
    That e'er on earth was born,

Although she wore Madonna's head
    And Venus' matchless form,
If e'er she'd yielded once her heart
    To other love than mine,
And, 'midst a thoughtless, wanton sport,
    Had quenched the flame divine.

A PASTORAL.

TRANSLATED FROM THE FRENCH OF HALLER.

The twinkling star descends at eve
   In trembling beams of light,
And from the mountain's purple brow
   Dispels the gloom of night.

The moon displays her silver horns
   In lightly shaded gleams,
And o'er the golden harvest sheds
   Her soft and tender beams.

And Night her sleepy odors spreads,
　　Her wat'ry pearls distills;
She kindly slakes the thirsty earth,
　　And feeds the fainting rills.

Come, Doris, let us wander out
　　Beneath the beechen shade,
And follow many a winding path
　　Along the grassy glade.

The zephyr breathes in amorous gales,
　　Along the distant grove,
And softly gives the tender leaves
　　A sweet caress of love.

See now, my Doris, yonder see
　　Yon bending willow's gloom,
Whose roots the murmuring waters lave,
　　Whose boughs look dark at noon.

And there, the leafy boughs among,

    We'll watch the turtle-doves;

We'll listen to their sweetest songs,

    And learn their tender loves.

And thus we'll nurse the growing thoughts,

    Remote from noise and strife;

Whilst ev'ry rural scene around

    Shall lend its sweets to life.

THE ADIEU.

Lady mine, I need not tell you
   What the tears of anguish spoke,
When my fainting eyes beheld you,
   As they gave the parting look.
In my bosom then were swelling
   Feelings such as none can tell,
As, with tongue and heart unwilling,
   Falt'ring sighed I, "Fare thee well."

Not my native land forsaking,
   Where my infant lot was cast,

Where a thousand scenes awaken
  Thoughts of friends and pleasures past;
Not to green and sunny bowers,
  Where my childish moments flew;
Not to pleasures, scenes, or flowers,
  Weeping, sighed I that adieu.

No, 'twas not companions leaving;
  No, 'twas not the sweets of home;
Which was in my bosom heaving,—
  'Twas the thoughts of *thee* alone.
Could I leave thee, vainly striving
  To conceal what sighs might tell?
Not without the keenest anguish,
  Could I utter, "Fare thee well."

LONELY MUSINGS.

I love to sit on the rugged cliff,
    Where the wild briers, clustering, spring;
Where naught but the reptile finds its home,
    And the eagle spreads its wing.
I love to gaze on the world below,
Where the forests wave and the waters flow,
Where the song of birds and the voice of men
Arise from the field, the wood, and the glen.

I love to sit on the mountain top,
    Where the sky is clear and bright,

And the stars pour down from their distant orbs
    Their silvery beams of light.
I love to gaze on the boundless scene,
And nurse in my mind the pleasing dream,
That those radiant spheres with life abound,
And joy and love and beauty are found.

I love to sit in the lonely vale,
    Where the shade hangs thick and dark;
Where the catbird builds and the owlet screams,
    And the whelps of the wild fox bark.
I love to sit in a lonely spot,
Where the mind can roam in the world of thought —
Within and without in beauty are joined
The world of matter and the world of mind.

"TELL HIM I'LL WAKE AGAIN."

A fair young female had just closed her eyes in her last repose. For many hours the spirit had been trembling within the expiring frame, like the blaze of a spent taper; for filial love, longing after the farewell of an absent father, still held it by strong ties. "Should you sleep when your father arrives, what shall I say to him?" a friend inquired significantly. The dying girl unclosed her fading eyes, and said with a gentle smile, "*Tell him I'll wake again.*" She slumbered, and woke no more.

> Tell him I'll wake again when morn
>   Sweet beams of light shall spread,
> And life's immortal day shall dawn
>   Upon the sleeping dead.

Tell him I'll wake in youthful bloom,
    All fresh and fair and bright;
No fell disease nor sorrow's gloom
    My rising joys shall blight.

Tell him this dying frame of mine
    Has wasted day by day,
Till, all unstrung, by slow decline,
    It hastens to decay.

Tell him, that still his dying child
    A father's love retained;
Though frail and weak, yet calm and mild,
    The goal of life she gained.

Tell him farewell, while I shall sleep;
    The morn will quickly come,
When I shall wake with joy to meet
    Him in our Father's home.

THE DAY OF BATTLE.

The morning star in beauty shone
  Along the dusky east;
Nor yet the purple light of dawn
  Had broke the slumberer's rest.

I gazed on woodland, hill, and plain,
  And all was peace around;
No voice of bird, no matin strain
  Of music yet was found.

The clear, bright arch of heaven above
    Hung o'er the silent scene;
Nor scarce a twig or leaflet moved,
    To break the fairy dream.

How sweet to me does nature seem,
    When thus alone we meet,
When earth is calm, and heaven serene,
    And every joy complete.

'T was sweet to muse, 't was sweet to feel,
    With star and bush and flower;—
When, lo! the flash, the cannon's peal
    Shook hill and plain and shore.

The shout, the cry, the sword, the drum,
    Now mix with horrid din;
And on the furious squadrons come,
    And death and carnage bring.

Now fire and smoke and death and groans
   At every step abound;
And blood and gore and shivered bones
   Bestrew the smoking ground.

The star has set — the morning sun
   Rose o'er a field of blood;
The hills and plains are black and dun,
   And leafless stands the wood.

Now all is still around, above,
   As when that star arose;
There is no voice that speaks of love;
   There's none that tells of foes.

But marks of rage on every side,
   And marks of savage man;
The signs of death are far and wide,
   And blood-stained is the land.

The leaf, the bud, the opening flower,
  Lie crushed upon the sand;
But coming time, with genial power,
  Will clothe anew the land.

The orphan's tear will dry again,
  And cease the widow's moans;
But when will spring or summer's voice
  Reclothe these bleaching bones?

NATURE A PROOF OF GOD'S EXISTENCE.

'Tis sweet to be alone, with nature's works
Around; where God has traced in clearer lines,
Than ever priest's or prophet's page contained,
The proofs of attributes divine; where earth
And heaven outstretch their ample page for man
To read. The humblest floweret of the vale,
If viewed aright, will prove to skeptic man
What never pagan rite, or papal bull,
Or mystic creed has proved, that God exists
In wisdom, power, and love — in all supreme.

For what, but wisdom infinite, could form
The simple leaf with varied hue, and filled
With countless tubes, that draw from earth's dark
 clods
A shapeless mass, dissolved and purified,
Till matter, brute and dead revives, and springs
To life, and crowns the vale with flowers and sweet
Perfumes? Can man such simple work perform?
The skillful hand may form a mimic rose,
With stem and leaf o'erspread with colors false,
And borrowed odors sweet. But let him bid
The organs play, its leaves unfold, and yield
Him incense, fresh and sweet at morn and eve,
As nature offers up to God. The rash,
Presumptuous man would stand abashed, and his
Own nothingness confess, compared with Him
Whose voice from nothing called to life, and clothed
With beauty all that lives.

WRITTEN ON ONE OF THE WESTERN MOUNDS.

> "They, who, adventurous, dare to tread
> 'Mid the dark dwellings of the dead,
> Shall learn the lessons fate has taught."

Amid the mounds I stand; the beech and oak

Trees wave their giant arms, branch above branch,

Moss-clad and gray with age, whilst deep beneath,

Their countless roots embrace a nation's bones.

But who? or when? 'tis secret all, unknown,

And locked amidst the gloom and darkness of

The dusky past. The grass has silently,
With flowers and leaves, its mantle spread, from year
To year, around their noiseless, populous
Abodes; the babbling stream, whilst nations, tribes,
And languages have sprung to life, enjoyed
Their day and died, has still, with ceaseless run,
Flowed by an empire's grave. How silent all!
No voice is here, except the wild bird's scream,
And the wolf's howl, to tell the unwritten tale.
And blank is history's garbled page, — not e'en
The deeds of blood and man's destroying might
Have stained the spotless scroll. Naught but the
    grave
Reveals the long-lost race, — a nobler race
Than now the red man boasts, — a race perhaps,
Who, ere the savage Greek had learned to spread
The tent or till the earth, had wooed the muse
In strains as sweet as ever Homer sung.

But earth itself has changed, and man's frail race,
Like autumn leaves, has oft been swept away
By tempest, flood, or storm; and ocean's bed,
Amid convulsions dire, upheaved, aloft
Its tow'ring peaks has reared; and, in their turn,
The mountain's dizzy height and outstretched plain
Deep in the yawning gulf have sunk, and o'er
Their tops the waves of ocean roll. Thus man
And man's proud works of monumental art,
Of sacred fanes and sculptured tombs, at one
Fell sweep, are swallowed up and lost. And age
On age rolls by; perhaps, not long before
The ebbing tide shall seek another bed,
And leave to man and beast a desolate
Abode. And then the curious eye will trace
Amid the upturned hills and plains, the wreck
Of races long since known on earth, as now
We view the mammoth's giant frame.

THE MIND UNCHANGEABLE.

"Forma mentis eterna."—Tacitus.

The fairest blossom of the spring,
    Though beautiful and gay,
The golden insect's gilded wing,
    Must quickly pass away.

The star of beauty shines on high,
    Whilst, o'er the mountain's height,
It climbs the dusky-bosomed sky,
    Amidst the lamps of night.

That star of beauty must decay,—
    Its course will soon be run;
The heavens and earth will pass away,
    When once their work is done.

Thus gilded wing and fairest flower
    And star must all decay;
But mind on heavenly wing will soar
    To an immortal day.

Forever there in spirit-land,
    Unchanged by lapse of time,
'T will all its various powers expand,
    And feed on truth divine.

MIND FEEDS ON THOUGHT.

What though the breath of heaven should fail,
Or fetid odors taint the gale;
Though earth refuse the mantling bower,
And mildews blast the opening flower;
Though nature's robe of living green
No longer spread o'er hill and plain,
But fen and marsh and drifting sand
Spread ruin o'er the sea and land;
Though moon and star and daily sun

No more their circling orbits run,
And darkness spread her sable wing
O'er man and every living thing;
And every outward sense grow dumb,
The eye be dark, and mute the tongue,—
Afar within itself retired,
The mind with heavenly vigor fired,
Could form anew the faded scene,
Blossom and herb and living green;
Could bid the zephyr's wing unfold,
And deck the clouds with fluid gold;
Could people space with star and sun,
And bid the fiery comet run;
Could soar away to spirit-lands
And dwell in thought with angel bands;
Or, backward, trace the track of man
To where his infant race began,
And there, in shrouds of darkness, find

The primal sparks of giant mind,
And every truth in nature trace
That e'er was known to human race.
And thus within itself alone,
Though every outward sense were gone,
The mind could live in heavenly light,
Where all is clear and fair and bright,
As when, a pure, immortal flame,
From God's own hand at first it came.

THE INDIAN.

He stood on the hill where his fathers had stood,
And gazed on the plains, the fields, and the wood;
But the smoke of the wigwam had faded in air,
And the shout of the warrior no longer was there.

The forests were gone, and the wild deer had fled;
The mounds were upturned that had covered the dead.
The stream and the lake still rose to his view,
Where the sport of his youth was the light bark canoe,—

But the track of the white man was seen on the shore;
In the field was his plough, in the stream was his oar;
And the flocks of the farmer were cropping their food,
Where the bark-covered hut of the warrior had stood.

Then, the last of the red men, he hastened away
From the graves where the bones of his forefathers lay,
To the grass-covered plains of the far distant West,
There alone in the desert unhonored to rest.

SCENES FROM A DREAM.

Sweetest flowers of lovely spring,
Singing birds with golden wing,
    Bloom and warble tuneful lays
Where in fancy's fabled bowers,
Where in hope's aspiring hours,
    Oft my soul with Delia strays.

By the streamlet's gentle flow,
Where the cress and cowslip grow,
    Where the zephyr has its home,
Where, in wild fantastic cell,

Silver-footed fairies dwell,
    I with Delia often roam.

Oft to view the craggy stone,
Mimic Echo's mossy throne,
    Oft to find the fabled grot,
Where, amid the gloom of night,
Once was seen the witch's light,
    I with Delia vainly sought.

Oft I've asked poetic fire,
Oft the lute and oft the lyre,
    Charming earth with angel's lay;
Dimly burned the poet's fire,
Dumb the lute, and dumb the lyre,
    When my Delia's far away.

Oft to view in dusky night,
Evening's robe of starry light,

Where the mighty planets ride,
Where the shooting meteors run,
Where the wandering comets burn,
  Oft I've gone by Delia's side.

When from life to shades of woe,
Pluto's realm of night below,
  I, a fancied spright, was driven,—
Then these dread abodes of hell,
Sinner's hut and devil's cell,
  Delia's presence turned to heaven.

When I roved through heavenly bowers,
Crowned with wreaths of deathless flowers,
  Sinless as the joys above;
Lone amidst the blest abodes,
Bowers of men and thrones of gods,
  Oft I mourned for Delia's love.

Oft I've strolled through Eden's bowers,
There to cull the bridal flowers,
  Then to wreathe them round her head;
When my joy had reached its height,
With the visions of the night,
  Then my Delia's image fled.

O'ER EGYPT'S PLAINS.

O'er Egypt's plains the heavens are bright,
   As when the Hebrews came,
And, 'mid the folds of pagan night,
   Lit up a heavenly flame.

And still the banks of Nile, the same,
   Still fanned by gentle winds,
As when old Pharaoh's daughter came
   To dip her snowy limbs.

Along its verdant banks of green,
   The wild flag rears its head,

As when the prophet's ark was seen,
   Amidst its waters laid.

There still a thousand sculptured cones,
   There still the Memnon stands;
But now their lofty pillared domes
   Protect the Arab bands.

But where, the Egyptian priest and lord?
   Where, Pharaoh's mighty son?
They smote the Jew — were cursed by God —
   And lo! their race is gone.

WHY PLUCK THE FLOWERS?

Why pluck the flowers of sweetest bloom,
   And spoil their opening hues,
Unless to taste their sweet perfume,
   And drink their nectar dews?

And why attempt, with impious art,
   To brand a fair one's name,
And often leave a broken heart
   To weep o'er injured fame?

Stay, vile deceiver, stay thy hand,
  Nor blast life's opening dawn;
Nor wreck young hope upon the strand
  Of wretchedness forlorn!

An artful look, or flattering smile,
  May pierce the tender heart;
Deceitful words allure with guile,
  And leave a deadly smart.

For woman's love is brittle ware,
  And broken by neglect;
And broken once, there's no repair
  Can heal the least defect.

THE WANDERER.

The dial's shade moves round and round,
And transient all on earth is found,
   And all is doomed to change.
The mountains waste, the rocks decay,
And men are dying every day
   Within this ample range.

The veil of Fate's before our eyes,
The future's hidden from the wise,

Uncertain what's to come.
Yet, we may view the fleeting past,
And scan our course from first to last,
  And think of what's been done.

Thus, as the banished man returns
And seeks his friends, but finds their urns,
  I viewed life's early morn;
I sought the pleasures once I knew,
And tried to bring again to view
  What long was past and gone.

Where, now, the trifling, rattling toy,
That once could please the smiling boy
  And still his whining cry?
Where, now, the borders of that span,
Where once he thought the earth began
  To mingle with the sky?

I sought the joys that once I knew,
I thought that I'd again pursue
   And taste their pleasures o'er.
I sought to find my native cot,
Those shattered rooms I'd not forgot,
   But that exists no more.

Its wretched tenants, now forlorn,
Had left it to the pelting storm,
   And sought a foreign clime;
Its tottering frame stood not the blast,
But tumbled to the ground at last,
   A mouldering wreck of time.

The wild weeds grew where once it stood;
The partridge nursed her infant brood
   Down where its ruins lay;
The tree that stood beside the door—

An autumn storm had blown it o'er —

Was mingling with the clay.

The little brook, whose murmurings stole

With raptures o'er my infant soul,

   Was lost in wilds of grass;

I traced its long forsaken stream,

Without the solace of a gleam

   Of where its waters passed.

The little warblers tuned their throats;

But theirs were wild and plaintive notes, —

   'T was not my robin's song;

For she was forced from hence away

To shun the savage birds of prey,

   In wretchedness to mourn.

I thought that these had passed away,

As doomed by nature to decay,

But else remained the same.
I asked where lived my little mates,
Who once with me did smile and prate,
And called them all by name.

A haggard form was standing near;
He pointed to a broken bier,
And answered with a sigh:
"Beneath yon grassy ridge of ground
The sleeping bones of one are found,
Of one to you most nigh.

"For once you knew her graceful form,
But ah, alas! the vernal storm
Has laid her in the tomb;
Her smiling lips and sparkling eyes,
And mind that once could charm the wise,
Are lost in death's dark gloom.

"Some, wandering, roam in foreign lands,
On Arctic's shores, on Afric's sands,
 And some on ocean's wave;
Whilst some have clothed themselves in shame,
And others reached the seats of fame,
 And some are in the grave."

I passed the street,—they knew me not,—
My boyish look they'd long forgot,
 And passed the stranger by.
Ye youthful scenes, while life remains,
Your cloudless joys I'll e'er retain
 Unmingled with a sigh.

THE MIND IS ETERNAL.

"Forma mentis eterna."— TACITUS.

Bowers of spring and groves of green,
Poet's home and fancy's dream,
  Wither in the scorching ray;
Blush of youth and smile of joy
Sorrow's dart may soon destroy;
  But the mind will ne'er decay.

Flowers that bloom and birds that sing,
Russet leaf and golden wing,

Quickly blossom, quickly fly;
Fashion's shine and folly's show
Often change to garbs of woe;
   But the mind will never die.

Golden ore and trump of fame,
Stores of wealth and honored name,—
   Useless glitter, empty sound;
Miser's hope and hero's dream,
Flitting shadows always seem;
   But of mind no end is found.

Pleasure's couch and Bacchus' bowl,
Bed of death and death of soul,
   Smile to win and win to slay.
But the mind will ever bloom,
Brighter yet beyond the tomb,
   Endless as eternal day.

A VISIT TO WASHINGTON.

What though I tread with wandering feet
    Potomac's winding shore;
What though I sit where sages meet
    And con their wisdom o'er: —
Yet still on fancy's wings I rise.
    In sweet, enchanting dreams.
To view my own New England skies,
    Her mountains, hills, and streams.

What though Virginia's mountains gleam
    Along the western sky,

And many a sacred grove is seen,
  Where Vernon meets the eye; —
Yet dearer far my native fields,
  Where once I loved to roam,
Whose dark-green grassy turf conceals
  The savage warrior's bones.

What though in sculptured walls still lives
  The hero's deathless name;
What though the faithful canvas gives
  The patriot's deeds to fame; —
Yet while I tread on Bunker's hill,
  And view the blood-stained fields,
A deeper flame my bosom fills
  Than e'er the canvas yields.

What though in marble-pillared halls,
  Beneath the gilded domes,

I see the gold-embroidered walls,
    And little mimic thrones;—
Oh, dearer far than seats of power,
    Or gilded wall and dome,
The grassy mound, the spreading bower,
    Around my cottage home!

What though the city belle may shine
    In beauty's gayest hue,
With rubies glittering from the mine,
    With garments ever new;—
The feeling heart, the gentler grace,
    The heavenly modesty,
The winning smile of Delia's face,
    Are dearer far to me.

HYMN FOR THE NEW YEAR.

How the silver spheres are rolling,
    Counting out life's transient span!
Who, their constant course beholding,
    Cannot tell, how frail is man?
Sun and moon, their course fulfilling,
    Tell the passing hour is gone;
Each the solemn truth revealing, —
    Soon their circling course is done!

See, as time is onward moving,
    Truth and Freedom spring to light;

Man, his social state improving,
>   From the tyrant claims his right.
See the light of reason shining
>   O'er delusion's misty way;
Pure religion undefiling,
>   Brightening into perfect day.

Every season yields its blessing,
>   Every year its bounty brings;
Man, alone these joys possessing,
>   Heeds not whence this goodness springs.
While in retrospect reviewing
>   What has marked our short career,
Still in virtue's path pursuing,
>   Let us hail the coming year.

THERE IS A WREATH.

'T is not of gold, nor yet of fame;
   'T is not entwined with beauty's name;
For gold grows dim, and beauty fades,
   And fame is lost 'midst gathering shades.

This wreath grows not in pleasure's bowers,
   Nor yet is formed of fading flowers;
Its deathless leaflets ever bloom,
   And shed their fragrance o'er the tomb.

'Tis virtue's prize, of heavenly worth,

Whose petals open here on earth,

But still in endless bloom will rise

Amid the bowers of Paradise.

DREAMING.

If we could avoid the painful and often heart-rending scenes which present themselves in the wild visions of sleep, and retain only those of joy and gladness, what an elysium of happiness there would be for the dreamer! No sooner would he close his eyes upon the toils and cares of the day, than he would find himself amidst the splendid creations of his own fancy, where joys were multiplied around him, and beauty was interwoven with every object. Reason is dethroned, and fancy reigns triumphant. We are no longer surprised by the strange and marvelous; time and space are annihilated; the events of years pass in as many moments; we are transported from place to place, without noticing the transition. The storehouse of memory is thrown open, and the forgotten events of a whole life are ransacked and brought forth in all their original freshness and vigor. Out of these, fancy creates a thousand fantastic combinations, often ludicrous and absurd; but delusion assumes the garb of reality, and the visions of fancy charm and delight us. Our days of childhood return; we again enjoy the sports that have long since been forgotten. Our companions are with us; the joy of youth is upon their countenance; time has written no wrinkle upon their brows; death has not thinned their ranks, nor sickness wasted their forms. They are *all* present.

Though many of them have long since mingled with the clods of the valley, the dreamer heeds it not; he has gone back to live again amidst the former scenes of life, and the present passes before his eyes like the shadowy images of prophetic vision. He tastes again the sweets of youthful love and affection, with the same ardor and transports as he did in the fire and artlessness of youth. He clasps the fairy form which he once adored; she is still clothed with youth and beauty. Awakening from such a rapturous vision of early life, he exclaims:—

> She lives in beauty fresh and fair
> As spring's most glorious morn;
> No length of years can e'er impair
> Her fancy-pictured form.
>
> Her voice is still as soft and sweet
> As childhood's accents flow;
> And artless joys upon her cheek,
> In smiles of gladness glow.
>
> With her I rove 'mid youthful scenes,
> And life's sweet morn renew;
> I heed it not, that only dreams
> Are present to my view.

WHAT I'VE SEEN.

I've seen the cradle and the grave,
Have seen the coward and the brave,
   On one low level lie.
I've seen the glittering wreath of fame;
Have seen it shrouded o'er with shame,
   And tinged with crimson dye.

I've seen the prince of royal blood,
Have seen the beggar asking food,
   By the same prince denied;

Again I've seen them in the tomb,
Wrapped in the self-same silent gloom,
   There lying side by side.

I've seen the rich with heaps of gold,
Have seen the slave for money sold,
   And fettered with a chain;
I've seen the slave man raised to wealth;
Have seen the rich one cold in death,
   'Mid heaps of rebels slain.

I've seen the rose and lily, torn
And beaten by the pelting storm,
   Lie withered in their bloom;
I've seen the fairest form on earth,
Upon the solemn sable hearse,
   Slow moving to the tomb.

THE PROGRESS OF SOCIETY.

A FRAGMENT.

My theme is man, 'tis mortal man I sing;
How first o'er brutal instinct placed; how rude
And wild the reasoning savage groped his way
Through dark and devious paths, ere long before
The star of knowledge rose to break the dawn
Of Wisdom's glorious day; how science led
The way to art, and knowledge taught the soul,
With outstretched wing and ceaseless flight t' explore
The mighty orb of nature's varied works.

Thou heavenly muse, who erst didst guide
The patriarch's pen, deep visioned in the past,
To trace the birth and rise of things, when first
Creative power from naught to being called
This mighty globe and all its sister orbs
That shine on high, inspire me now with light
Divine to trace in man the kindling spark
Of intellect, that greatest, holiest gift
Of God, implanted deep in man, t' adorn
And finish still, what God of all his works
Alone imperfect left, the human mind.
For thou canst tell how all the mighty powers
And restless energies, concealed and veiled in flesh,
Were wed to Adam's dust, and mortal with
Immortal natures joined; how spirit clad
In robes of earth can act through organs so
Obtuse, or else by its own power can purge
The grosser part, till matter spirit seems.

Say first of our great parent sire, when at

Creation's morn, unstained by sin, he first

In Eden's bowers sweet converse held with God,

Or walked with angel bands to pluck the flowers

And breathe the fragrant gales, that played o'er hill

And vale; or else with Eve, sweet partner of

His sweetest joys, retired beneath the shade

Of overhanging vines, he passed away

His happy hours. What powers, what intellect,

What stretch of thought were his? Had knowledge dawned

And with bright orient beam illumed his soul?

Was sacred truth revealed, and nature's course

With all her wonder-working laws to him

Apparent made? Not so; for scarcely, then,

Had human powers to brutal instinct soared.

For God, at first, to all the countless tribes

Which people earth and air and sea, had given
That sure, unerring guide, a sense unknown
Or feebly felt in man, but to all else
In measure full and perfect given. On man
Was mind bestowed, not full, not perfect made
At first, but feeble, as the tender plant
Whose future form is yet concealed within
The parent bud, which showers and genial rains
Must nourish into life. So mind was left,
Imperfect, undeveloped, and untaught,
And man enjoined to rear and fashion it
With constant toil and sacred truth, until
Its latent powers break forth, its energies
Unfold, and every art and knowledge too
Be comprehended in its grasp. So our
Great sire, in intellect, was as the child
That prattles round the parent knee and seeks
For knowledge as for food from those who gave

It birth. With him began that mighty stream
Of wisdom's treasured lore, which age on age
Has swelled until it flows o'er earth, as o'er
Its bed the ocean sweeps with restless wave.

TO DELIA.

Though thine eyes as brilliants sparkle,
Though thy lips with rubies vie,
'T is not lips that vie with rubies,
Nor the lustre of thine eye;
No, 't is not that sweet complexion,
Blushing brighter than the rose,
Nor thy gently heaving bosom,
Whiter than descending snows;
'T is not all those witching graces,
That around thee ever play,

Nor thy voice so sweetly warbling
Many a soft and pensive lay;
Charms all these, far, far surpassing,
Prompt the soft and secret sigh,
Wake the soul to love and honor, —
Truth and Sensibility.

WE SEE NO HOSTILE BLADE.

Written for a celebration of the payment of the last dollar of the national debt during the administration of Gen. Jackson.

We see no hostile blade,
   No crimsoned banner o'er us;
We sit in Freedom's shade,
   Her altar stands before us.
     For all our rights
     Old Hick'ry fights,
Our Constitution still sustaining;
     Our deeds of fame,
     Our honored name,
With constant care maintaining.

WE SEE NO HOSTILE BLADE.

When Britain's hostile fleet
   Hung threat'ning on our border;
When *trait'rous* bands did meet
   To spread around disorder;
     He clasped the shield,
     And, in the field,
Their ranks he rent asunder;
     With brother's care,
     He saved the *Fair*,
And trod the blood-hounds under.

He quits the tented fields,
   Forgets the roaring cannon,
And reason's weapons wields
   Against the king of Mammon.*
     With mighty hand,
     He saved the land,

---

* The old U. S. Bank.

And from her chains unbound her;
Sweet peace he shed,
And plenty spread,
And blessings strewed around her.

Our nation's free, is free!
No foeman to invade her;
Our land's at liberty
From *debts* that would degrade her.
And every chain
We'll break in twain,
Whilst Jackson holds his station.
So then we'll see
A people free,
A free and happy nation.

MIGNON.

FROM THE GERMAN OF GOETHE.

Knowest thou the land where the citrons bloom;
The gold orange shines in its leafy gloom,
And softer the breeze from the blue heaven blows,
The myrtle still and the high laurel grows, —
Knowest thou it well? Oh, there! Oh, there!
Might I with thee, my true love, repair.

Knowest thou the house, with its pillared domes,
Its glittering halls and its gilded rooms?
The marble forms there seem to say,
"What ails thee, poor child?" as they look on me.

Knowest thou it well? Oh, there! Oh, there!
Might I with thee, my protector, repair.

Knowest thou the Alps, in their misty shroud?
The mule seeks his path through the midst of the
    cloud;
In the caverns the old dragon nourishes her brood;
The rocks tumble down, and o'er them the flood.
Knowest thou it well? Oh, there, with thee,
Where leads the way, O father, let us flee!

THE WANDERER'S LOT.

The wanderer's life I envy not,
Nor wish to share his changing lot;
His toilsome path, his glory, fame,
To me are but an empty name.
From country, friends, and sacred home,
Oh, who would ever wish to roam?
What though he cross the briny deep,
Or climb the mountain's rugged steep,
And stand on Andes' peerless height
Amid the cloudless fields of light;

Or else from Atlas' summit trace
The swarthy tribes of Afric's race;
Or madly urged, with daring soul,
O'er Baffin's ice to seek the pole?
What though he muse in classic lands
Where many a ruined temple stands,
Where many a sculptured form divine
Still mocks the wasting hand of time,
And still in beauty greets the eye
Of every careless passer-by?
What though on Zion's holy hill
Amid the pilgrim bands he kneel,
Where once the Hebrew prophets stood
Around the sacred ark of God?
What though the banks of Nile he tread
And seek through desert sands its head?
What though his devious steps pursue,
From land to land, a something new,

Till all his sands of life have run;
Till, worn and weary and alone,
Amid some trackless desert's gloom
He find at last a nameless tomb?
No father's hand, no mother's care,
No weeping wife or child is there
To calm his aching brows to rest,
And soothe the anguish of his breast;
But savage woods and savage lands,
And savage beasts and savage men,
Are what his devious steps have sought,
Are all the wealth his life has bought.

NEW YEAR'S ADDRESS.

The enameled robe of leaf and bud and flower,
Which spreads o'er hill and dale and vernal bower,
When spring, with breezy breath and balmy beam,
Sheds life and joy on mountain, plain, and stream;
The darker, richer hues of summer's shroud,
Her matin song of birds, her evening cloud;
The russet leaf of autumn's golden day,
That marks the hast'ning footsteps of decay, —
Alike have marked the seasons' circling round,
And told *another* year its final bound.

'T is thus we note mysterious time's career,

From change to change, and measure out the year;

While through the vistas of departed day,

Age rolls o'er age, in long and dread array.

But if time's lengthened years we view,

And trace man's upward course anew;

How first, with brutes, in tree and den,

Contented dwelt the savage man;

And how, when infant art had taught

To rear himself a cheerless cot,

Far worse than beasts that roam the wood,

He dipped his hands in brother's blood,

And then himself became a *god;*

How superstition held confined

That heavenly spark, the human mind,

And bade it trace its wondrous birth

To gods, the reptiles of the earth;

How, when the star of promise rose,
With life bright-beaming in its ray,
And to our darkened race disclosed
The dawn of an eternal day;
How superstition reared its head,
And round the soul its darkness spread;
While priest and monk and nun unite
To quench the dawning beams of light;
Retracing thus, 'tis wise to see
How man, how mind, how thought, is free, —
How free from foes, whose direful aim
Was still to load us with their chain.

Who taught the infant arts to man?
Who led him from his savage den?
Who bade his feeble powers expand,
His mind to guide the skillful hand
To rear aloft the sculptured piles,
Whilst Nature from the canvas smiles?

Who winged with mighty power the soul,

To tread the heavens from pole to pole,

To trace the comet's devious way,

Through realms of night — through realms of day,

And then survey, in space unknown,

The dazzling suburbs of His throne?

Who hung these orbs of glittering light

Along the curtained folds of night?

Again we ask, who taught the mind,

Its fetters burst, and unconfined,

From abject ignorance to rise,

And, winged with science, tread the skies;

This mortal form to consecrate

To civil life, and moral state?

'T was godlike Reason, all proclaim,

That living spark of heavenly flame,

God's greatest gift; on man bestowed

To mark him chief, creation's lord;

And by its feeble, glimmering ray,
To give a foretaste of that day
When knowledge, all unveiled and free,
Through the bright portals of eternity,
Shall pour upon the mind.

Who then shall say, with impious word,
That Reason's voice shall not be heard,
But some mysterious influence given
Shall guide our upward path to heaven?
Though dark such mystic power may seem,
Yet *darker* still will be the dream,
When once we wake to Reason's light,
And backward view the illusive night
Of lengthened shadows as they roll,
Which *craft* has spread around the soul.

Come, sacred Reason, heavenly ray,
Come, mighty Truth, and guide my way.

I ask no art, no mystic creed of man,

That's formed by few — *and fewer understand.*

A perfect form of perfect life we have,

The spotless model that the SAVIOR gave;

A life like his, of good, of love to man,

Far more avails than popish *dogmas* can.

And who by such a rule his life shall lead,

Will all the forms of mystic faith exceed;

Nor rests his claim to heaven on *rites* alone,

The life he leads conducts him safely home.

No pious hates within his bosom roll,

But truth and justice stand around his soul.

His every *act* proclaims his heavenly birth,

And speaks "*good-will to man and peace on earth.*"

Next Knowledge, reason's richest fruit,

Exalts the man above the brute;

Exalts the soul, its powers unbinds,

And yields its treasures to our minds.

It frees from superstition's sway,
Where specters stand in long array;
Where witch, and ghost, and fairy bands
Still live, the gift of pagan hands;
Where *miracles* are falsely claimed,
And *inspiration's* gifts profaned.
When Knowledge pours its sacred light,
In haste these phantoms take their flight,
And leave the mind, in Nature's laws,
For all effects to find a cause.

As Knowledge beams upon our age,
The skeptic's doubts, the bigot's rage,
Like stingless serpents turn and flee,—
For Error's weak, *where Reason's free!*
But oft beneath the bigot's frown,
Has Reason's sacred voice been drowned;
And Knowledge, Science, all
Enclosed within the cloistered wall.

Yet Reason triumphs o'er their rage;

And Knowledge beams upon our age.

Religion free, from dogmas free,

From creeds and crowns and Holy See,

As Heaven directs, by Reason's light,

Herself will purge from pagan rite.

Religion pure, of holy birth,

Was formed for man, *for man on earth;*

His duty to his fellow, kindly given,

To form on earth a race for heaven.

And yet in these enlightened days

Are found those pious Pharisees

Who teach, religion not in deeds

Consists, but more in mystic creeds,

Where blind belief is all in all.

Year steals on year with noiseless feet;

Their endless course the seasons keep;

To some with joys they overflow;

To some they bring a load of woe;

To some, the bridal's joyful boon;

To some, the darkness of the tomb,—

And all who now behold the day

Will, in their turn, be swept away.

Then while we greet the *coming year*

With ardent hope and festive cheer;

While fancy to our eager sight

Unfolds the scene, as fair and bright,

'T is wise for us to turn, indeed,

And in the *past* the *future* read.

But while we live, to one great end,

May all our acts and efforts tend,

To serve our God by serving man;

And thus promote the general plan

Of Universal Good.

1835.

GREECE.

"'T is Greece; but living Greece no more." — BYRON.

The laurel grows on Sparta's plains
   With boughs as fresh and green,
As when among her warlike trains
   Leonidas was seen.
But 'neath its shade the cringing slave
Now only seeks a coward's grave.

The olive crowns her mountain caves,
   Where men communed with gods;
His flowery banks Eurotas laves
   Where Sparta's daughters trod.

Now robbers haunt these sacred shades,
And Turks enslave the Grecian maids.

O'er Lacedæmon's ruined wall
   The skies are soft and blue;
And on her fields there nightly falls
   A sweet and heavenly dew;
But Ceres finds no priesthood* there,
Nor heeds the Moslem's faithless prayer.

The hills, the fields, and rolling streams,
   The mountain's waving woods,
So fair, so bright, so sweet, they seem
   The blest abodes of gods;
But where the godlike Spartans now,
That laid the Persian millions low!

       * Husbandmen.

1834.

THE MOUNTAIN SHEPHERD'S SONG.

FROM THE GERMAN OF UHLAND.

I dwell on the mountain tops,
   And gaze on the towers below;
Here the sun first shines on the rocks;
   Here the evening sunbeams glow.

Here the streamlets and fountains rise;
   I drink them fresh from their source;
The mist dashes up to the skies,
   As they rush o'er the rocks in their course.

THE MOUNTAIN SHEPHERD'S SONG.

The cliff is the home of my youth;
  In its wrath the storm rages round,
It howls from the north to the south,
  Its fury my song shall outsound.

The thunders roll under my feet,
  As I stand in the midst of the sky;
I see where the broad flashes meet,
  And bid them pass harmlessly by.

But soon as the war-trumpets blow,
  And fires are seen from afar,
I descend to the valleys below,
  To sing the loud death-song of war.

SPRING.

How sweet is the first approach of spring,
   When the birds and flowers return;
When the lark and the red-breast sing,
Or fan the air with their gilded wing,
   And the wild rose opes to the sun.

How sweet is the morning fresh with dew,
   While the zephyrs play around;
When the flowers their richest fragrance strew,
When the air is soft and the sky is blue,
   And beauty clothes the ground.

How sweet, how short, are our youthful dreams,
   When the thoughts are light and gay;
When the cheek is bright and the young eye beams,
When love in the bosom but faintly gleams,
   And hope is as bright as day.

How sweet and pure are the thoughts at death,
   When the sins are all forgiven;
When we breathe with joy our latest breath,
Nor care for the fleeting things of earth,
   But hasten away to heaven.

HOPE.—TO MARY.

WRITTEN IN AN ALBUM.

Mary, the night may look black,
   With clouds, with tempest and storm;
But hope cheers the traveler's track,
   With the speedy approaches of morn.

Mary, the shadows of woe
   May threaten to burst on our head;
But sweeter the transports shall flow,
   When the anguish of sorrow is fled.

HOPE.—TO MARY.

Mary, misfortune may spread,
  O'er the prospects of youth, its dark shroud;
But hope in its brightness will shed
  Its sweet beams of joy o'er the cloud.

Mary, th' affections of youth,
  And the soft smile of friendship may die;
But hope, like the fountains of truth,
  Flows down from regions on high.

Mary, though life, like a flower,
  May wither and fade in its bloom;
Hope points to a bright sunny bower,
  Through shadows that hang o'er the tomb.

THE GRAVEYARD.

On the farther side of a rugged hill,
Is a piece of ground with dead bones filled;
'T is enclosed by wall of small grey stones,
As a burying place for human bones.

The beech and the birch trees' spreading shade
Lies cool on the turf where the graves are made;
And the crippled fern rears its lowly head,
As it creeps o'er the dust of the sleeping dead.

The sculptured slab or the humbler stone
Marks the length and breadth of the narrow home;
And the name of the sleeper is still to be seen,
Though the gathering moss on its face looks green.

There the tall grass bends o'er the broken bier,
Where scarcely the signs of a grave appear;
But the marks of the mourner's frequent step
Still show where the true one has often wept.

Here the infant, snatched from its mother's breast,
And the aged man and matron rest;
Here the laughing child and the hoary head
Together meet in the realms of the dead.

Here's the man from the midst of active life,
With his sleeping babes and a lovely wife;
And here in the grave was lately laid
The faded form of a blooming maid.

But 't is said that the mind has flown away,
Through the boundless realms of space to stray;
That it wings its way to the distant spheres,
And lives through the endless flow of years.

But sure 't will return again to earth,
And gaze on the scenes of its early birth;
'T will sigh in the gale as it passes by,
Or smile in the golden tints of the sky.

Sure it will stoop to the flowery glade,
Where its early footsteps often strayed;
Or sit by the side of the bubbling streams,
And joyfully muse o'er its youthful dreams.

AN IMITATION OF MIGNON.

Knowest thou the land, where the wild savage dwells?
There the war-song is sung, and the red warrior yells;
There the hut of the chieftain is painted with blood,
And the maiden flies swift in her boat o'er the flood.
Knowest thou the land? Oh, there! Oh, there!
My true love, my true love, O let us repair.

Knowest thou the wood, where the tall cedar grows?
There the queen of the rivers majestically flows,

AN IMITATION OF MIGNON.

The streamlet and fountain roll down to the plain,
Long wand'ring and winding they seek for the main.
Knowest thou the wood? Oh, there! Oh, there!
My true love, my true love, O let us repair.

Knowest thou the prairies, the plains and the meads?
There tall grows the grass, where the buffalo feeds;
The wild ox is seen on the banks of the stream,
Where the bright specks of gold thro' the dark waters gleam.
Knowest thou the land? Oh, there! Oh, there!
My true love, my true love, O let us repair.

Knowest thou the far, the far distant West?
There spring with her roses forever is drest;
There summer eternal pours music divine;
There autumn and harvest unceasingly shine.
Knowest thou it well? Oh, there! Oh, there!
My true love, my true love, O let us repair.

AN IMITATION OF MIGNON.

Knowest thou the path? There the fire-breathing boat
Moves swift on its way with its flames and its smoke,
Not an oar nor a sail, not a sheet nor a shroud,—
It glides on its way like the shade of a cloud.
Knowest thou the way? Oh, now! Oh, now!
My true love, my true love, O now let us go.

IF I WERE A CHILD.

If I were a child I'd sport and play;
    I'd rove through woods and fields;
I'd pluck the earliest flowers of May,
    And drink the sweets they yield.

I'd sit by the side of the babbling brook,
    As the zephyrs passed along;
I'd hide in the alders' shady nook,
    And mock the red-breast's song.

IF I WERE A CHILD.

I'd find where the painted rainbows rise,
    And chase them from morn till noon;
By night I'd watch at the foot of the skies,
    And catch the rising moon.

I'd seek where the sweetest wild flowers blow;
    I'd find where the streamlets run;
In the meadows I'd find where the fox-gloves grow,
    The tall wild grass among.

I'd make me wings to fly in the air;
    I'd rise at the break of day,
And catch the larks that were singing there;
    And drive the hawks away.

I'd build me a boat, a jolly boat,
    As light as the lightest feather;
And on the dancing waves I'd float
    In the bright and sunny weather.

If I were a child how sweet 't would be
    To prattle and laugh and play;
Then at eve to be rocked on my mother's knee,
    And sleep my cares away.

THE MOUNTAIN SHEPHERD.

My home is on the mountain tops;
    I rove around their sides;
I dwell among the cliffs and rocks,
    Where gushing fountains glide;
By day I watch my grazing flocks,
    By night in caverns hide.

When morn first sheds its purple light
    Along the dusky east,

High on the mountain's peering height
    Its kindling azure rests;
Whilst, o'er the plains, retiring night
    Still spreads her gloomy vest.

And still the lingering sunbeam plays,
    My caverned halls among;
Whilst thro' their crystal arches strays
    The shepherd's evening song;
With golden light the mountains blaze,
    And fading day prolong.

Beneath my feet the storm-clouds roar;
    The forked lightnings shine;
Whilst heaven's bright beams in sweetness pour
    Around this home of mine;
Here, safe above, I'm smiling o'er
    This raging scene sublime.

The lark flies up to meet, with me,
    The beams that morning sheds;
Whilst o'er the fields a vapor-sea
    Its fleecy foldings spreads;
Where flower and shrub and tow'ring tree
    Rear up their dewy heads.

AN EVENING SKETCH.

MEMORY AND HOPE.

Now the gold-bespangled West
    Hangs its curtained folds on high;
Now sweetly sinks the sun to rest
    Adown the western sky;
While thought rolls back to meet the morn
And tread anew the dewy lawn,
Where incense-breathing zephyrs play,
And rosy light leads in the day.

Twilight spreads its dusky rays
  Darkly o'er the village green;
Whilst Memory backward fondly strays
  Through life's gay fleeting dream;
And fresh o'er fancy's mirrored glass
The fleeting forms of childhood pass—
Though long, long fled from human eye,
These cherished scenes can never die.

Memory spreads her magic wing
  O'er the hurrying stream of time,
And on the distant shadows flings
  The rays of light divine.
I see the distant mansion rise,
Where day first met my infant eyes;
I walk along its antique halls,
And gaze upon its sculptured walls.

Now, in distant prospect seen,
   Childhood's artless, busy throng
Are sporting round the little green
   The aged trees among.
There Fancy's eye can fondly trace
A former friend in every face;
But now, alas, how few remain!
How few on earth will meet again!

Lovely vision, stay, O stay!
   ·Fairest of the youthful fair;
Thy cheek was brighter than the day,
   "More beautiful than air."
Ere Memory learned her magic art,
Thy image dwelt within my heart;
And long the sacred pledge was given,
Ere Fate recalled thee back to heaven.

Visioned forms before me rise;
    Youthful pleasures live in air;
When reason wakes, delusion flies,
    And leaves me in despair.
The shades of night around me fly;
Her pale, dim lamps are hung on high;
But in the dusky-bosomed East,
The promised star of morning rests.

Soon the circlet of the morn,
    O'er the mountain's peering height,
Shall spread the fleecy robes of dawn
    And breathe the purple light;
So, when a transient joy is past,
Its baseless form eludes our grasp;
But far beyond the fleeting dream,
Hope sheds its soft and heavenly beam.

AN EVENING SKETCH.

Yonder, heaven's ethereal bow
   Arches o'er the distant glade —
In vain the thoughtless lads pursue
   The illusive phantom's shade;
What is 't that charms th' enraptured sight?
'T is Hope's bright ray of sacred light;
Whilst o'er the future's distant scenes,
It shines with kind, inviting beams.

Gathering clouds obscure the morn;
   Deep and dark their drap'ry folds;
But ere they meet the mid-day sun,
   Away their vapor rolls;
So, on the present clouds of woe,
Sweet Hope erects her glittering bow;
And far beyond the yawning tomb,
She waves her light, fantastic plume.

Death may snatch the loveliest form,
    Angel of our youthful love:
But Hope can raise her from the tomb,
    Through fancy's realms to rove.
There Hope prolongs the fleeting hour;
There freshly rears the nuptial bower:
And there it spreads, in endless bloom,
A sinless Eden's sweet perfume.

THE GHOST STUDENT.

FROM THE GERMAN OF GOETHE.

My old ghost-master's far away,
And all his sprites shall me obey;
I've watched his charms, I've watched his art,
With which he bade the goblins start;
And now, with spirit-power, I'll show
  What magic wonders I can do.
    Hasten! Hasten!
    Quick be going,
    Let the water's
    Stream be flowing;

Let the current running in,
Fill the bath unto the brim.

Come, now, old Besom, stand upright,
For many a time you 've been a knight —
With head above, on two legs stand —
Put on your dress with hasty hand —
Take pail or pot, obey my will,
And tubs and bath and basin fill.
Hasten! Hasten!
Quick be going,
Let the water's
Stream be flowing;
Let the current running in,
Fill the bath unto the brim.

Away he goes to yonder stream;
Already there, and here again —

THE GHOST STUDENT.

He's gone again, again is here,
And foaming full the baths appear;
Away again — he's here with more —
The vessels all are running o'er.

    Slacken! Slacken!
    In abundance
    Thy rich gifts are
    All around us —
    Ah! I mark it — I've forgotten,
    How the magic charm is broken!

Alas! the word he uses when
He'd change the demon back again —
Oh that thou wast a lifeless broom!
He's bringing yet! he fills the room!
The cellar's full! the house's o'erflowing!
And still the hellish thing is going.

    I no longer
    Can endure it;

> Could I seize him,
>
> He should rue it —
>
> See, ah, see him fiercely staring!
>
> See his demon eyeballs glaring!

Alas, thou imp of Satan's brood,
Shall the house become a flood?
In every room I see it pour;
The stream is now above the floor;
And still the goblin hears me not,
But fills again his waterpot.

> Now I'll end thee,
>
> Wicked demon;
>
> And no longer
>
> Shalt thou be one —
>
> But with blow of dashing thunder,
>
> I'll cleave thy wooden head asunder.

See, again he's on his track;
I'll try the axe upon his back —

Stop there, I say — 't was bravely done!
He's lying now upon the ground —
In two his mangled form I see —
Again I've hope, again I am free.
 Wonder! Wonder!
 All surprising!
 Both the fragments,
 See them rising!
 Lo! they stand, like towering knight,
 Two in numbers, two in might.

Wet and wetter! both are running —
With flowing pails again they're coming.
With water, water, water all,
The cellar's full, and full the hall:
O lord and master! 'hear me call.
Ah, there he comes — the master's here —
His mystic words the demons hear.

" In thy corner,

Besom, Besom,

Quick retiring,

For a season,

Wait the charm that now controls you —

Wait the call of him who holds you."

THEY CALL ME INFIDEL.

They call me infidel; yes, they who trust
To formal creeds, and shadowy rites performed;
To low, debasing fear, and look demure;
To prayers of priests; to sermons saintly said, —
To wash away their sins, and make amends
For wrongs and daily outrage done to man;
Who feigned repentance bring, to cloak their deeds
Of shame, and hope 't will stand instead of works
Of moral worth, and duties well performed,
The pure and holy deeds of charity,

The tender love embracing all in one,
And binding man to man, with kindred ties
Of mutual zeal and universal good;
Who, chained to forms and rites can never feel
That high and godlike stretch of thought,
Which wings the infant mind for heaven;
Or, patient toiling here on nature's page,
Is ever searching deep for wisdom's lore.
But let these saintly men, in contrast, bring
Their formal acts of cold, unfelt devotion,
And, with the glowing, heartfelt admiration
Of nature's child, compare *their* languid zeal.
Enclosed with walls of wood and brick and stone,
Adorned with painted saints, or martyred forms
Of priests and popes, *they* vainly worship God.
Beneath the starry canopy of heaven,
The soft blue sky inlaid with countless gems
Of richer worth than gold or diamond's shine,

Where roll the radiant orbs which rise and set,
Obedient to the will of Him who lit
Their silver lamps and bade them shine, — beneath
This star-bespangled fane, my altars rise.
The mountains' peering tops, whose snowy heads,
Commingling with the clouds, look out on heaven;
The everlasting hills, deep-pillowed in the womb
Of earth, where playful nature fashions out
The shadowy forms of all that be on earth,
In air, or ocean's wave, which, raised above,
Instinct with life and being, move; the shore,
Where beat the restless wave and rolling tide;
The wide extended plains and desert sands,
Where fiery winds their baleful empire hold,
The altars these whereon my soul pours out,
In deep and heartfelt thought, her adoration.
I trace the hand divine, in every link
Of being's endless chain. As well may God

Be seen in earth, as heaven; the lowliest flower
That decks the vale, the feeblest insect form,
As plainly speaks of God, as man, or high
Angelic race. The sun, the rain, the earth,
The balmy air, invigorates and warms
The slimy reptile tribes, as well as kings,
And popes, and sanctimonious priests,
Who think that heaven and earth were made for them,
And hell for all besides.

MAN AND WOMAN.

FROM THE GERMAN OF SCHILLER.

WOMAN.

Here's honor to woman; I sing of her worth;
The roses of heaven she scatters on earth;
In the bonds of her love she enraptures the heart;
   'Neath the veil of her beauty and honor combined,
   She nurses a flame of the holiest kind,
The kindliest love with the kindliest art.

MAN.

Ever from the bounds of truth,

Strays the restless mind of man;

Now he's tossed on passion's sea,

Now he's wrecked on passion's strand —

Never rests his restless heart;

Wandering oft thro' distant scenes, —

Now along the starry vault,

Run his wild, fantastic dreams.

WOMAN.

But woman, with magical sweetness divine!

How softly she calls back the wanderer's mind,

And warns him to seek, in her presence, repose;

  In the hut of a mother, how modest and fair,

  The daughters are reared with the tenderest care;

Whilst the blossoms of virtue are twined with the

    rose.

MAN.

Fiendlike are the works of man,
Blood and slaughter mark his way;
Through the maze of life he runs,
Restless as the fleeting day —
What he rears, again destroys;
Endless war his wishes wage,
Never, like the hydra's heads,
Cease to rise with triple rage.

WOMAN.

But silently woman is seeking her fame;
The gaze of the eye is the height of her aim;
With industrious care she pursues her design,
    For she's freer than man from the pressures of life,
And freer than his are her wishes from strife,
Whilst the round of her goodness is endless as time.

MAN.

Strong and proud and fond of self,

Man's cold bosom never knows

(Fondly clinging round the heart,)

Half the joys of godlike love;

Never knows the exchange of soul;

Never pours the melting tears;

Harder than his hardened heart

Every tender thought he sears.

WOMAN.

As the light wing of zephyr, now fluttering along,

Breathes soft through the harp the Æolian song,

So the soul of a woman breathes music divine.

At the shadow of sorrow she softens to tears;

Her bosom is moved with tenderest fears,

And her eye with the dew-drop of pity will shine.

MAN.

But in man's tyrannic sway,

Power's the rule of right;

Scythia's sword now rules the day,

Persia's sons are slaves at night —

Direful passions shake his frame;

Wild and rough are his desires;

Discord rears her horrid voice;

Peace in wild affright retires.

WOMAN.

But woman, with soft and persuasive request,

Enjoys her dominion and rules in the breast;

She hushes contention and strife into peace;

  She softens the brave, the coward reproves;

  She mantles her cheek with the smiles of her love,

Recalling our wanderings, she bids them to cease.

NOT GLORY'S PLUME.

Not glory's plume nor beauty's ray,
    Nor sordid riches given,
Can light the soul's benighted way
    And lead it up to heaven.

Religion seeks her wandering guest,
    Amid life's tempests driven;
And on her calm and peaceful breast,
    She bears it up to heaven.

Then what is wealth, and what is fame,
　Or smiling beauty, even?
They're but a phantom, but a name,
　That never leads to heaven.

LINES WRITTEN IN A YOUNG LADY'S ALBUM AT SCHOOL.

When life's young morn shall fade in years,

And blooming youth in age appears;

When o'er these classic walls shall twine

The gathering moss and clustering vine;

When those who trod these halls with you,

In various climes their course pursue;

Whose youthful forms no room can find

Amid the cares that fill your mind, —

Then on these pages you may view

The pale, dim names that once you knew.

Our cheeks, though now in rosy health,
Will then, perhaps, be cold in death;
Or living, still there'll scarce remain
On memory's page one lingering name.
If then these lines you chance to see,
Inscribed on friendship's page to thee,
Remember well that he, who framed
These simple rhymes, your friendship claimed.

ON RECOVERING FROM SICKNESS.

FROM THE FRENCH OF GRISSET.

O day of sweet recovering health!
    Bright hours of joyful mirth!
It is a ray of heavenly life;
    A new restoring birth.
What pleasures kindle in my breast
To view the purple curtained west,

ON RECOVERING FROM SICKNESS.

    As twilight fades away.
The meanest object strikes my view;
To me the universe is new,
    And all is fair and gay.

The dewy, verdant groves among,
    When golden morn appears,
The wakeful linnet's matin song,
    With transport strikes my ears;
A thousand sights now meet my eye,
Which oft had passed unheeded by;
    But now their charms I see.
Sweet sights to vulgar eyes unseen,
With winning look and gentle mien,
    Are ever new to me.

ON THE DEATH OF A YOUNG LADY.

The floweret bloomed in the breath of morn,
   With its gems of pearl and dew,
And oped to the breeze its painted form
   Its petals of golden hue.

But the spoiler seized its robes of green,
   Whilst he plucked its golden crest;
And the worm and the reptile soon were seen
   In riot on its breast.

So Delia's heart beat high, and hope was bright,
    As the dreams of youth passed by;
Her cheek was red and her step was light,
    As her fancied joy drew nigh.

But her hopes and dreams have quickly passed,
    And her glass of life is run;
Whilst death in his icy arms has clasped
    Her cold and lifeless form.

And oft shall the rose and wild flower bloom,
    And oft the spring return;
But the sleep of death, in the cold damp tomb,
    Shall rest o'er her silent urn.

But 'tis said that the mind shall never die;
    That it dwells no more on earth;
But roams through the bright and boundless sky,
    Away from the place of its birth.

THE ONE WHO IS FAR AWAY.

'T was at the dusky hour of night;
The trembling star was clear and bright;
When, as I watched its feeble ray,
I thought of her who 's far away.

And far on high the silver moon
Had slowly reached its nightly noon;
When thus its crescent seemed to say,
"I look on her who 's far away."

When thus a heathen's prayer I prayed,
And humbly asked for Luna's aid;

THE ONE WHO IS FAR AWAY.

O speak, indulgent queen, I pray,
And tell of her, who's far away.

Say, does she watch thy ceaseless run,
From dusky eve till rise of sun?
And does she never seem to say
A word of him, who's far away?

O Luna, from thy throne above,
Reflect *her* image, whom I love;
And let me see, till dawn of day,
A glimpse of her who's far away.

A DREAM.

FROM THE SPANISH.

I saw a flower, — alone it bloomed,
    Ungathered and unsought;
I stretched my hand to grasp its stem,
    But ah! I reached it not.

Between us flowed a dusky stream,
    Unfathomed and unknown;
And on its distant banks there stood
    This beauteous flower alone.

But summer's suns and thirsty winds
   Drank up the lessening stream;
And now between its grassy banks
   Was but a brooklet seen.

That flower still stood in beauty's bloom,
   Ungathered and alone:
With eager hand, I seized the stem,
   And lo! 'twas all my own.

WRITTEN IN AN ALBUM.

Sacred page, bright virgin leaf,
   Yet unsullied by a stain;
Thine to keep for joy or grief
   Friendship's brightest, holiest flame.

Picture fit of life's young morn;
   When, as yet unstained by sins,
Love and hope and peace are born,
   And our joyous life begins.

Sacred page to friendship's name,
    Ne'er receive the flatterer's pen;
Nobler thoughts thy bosom claim,
    Waking mem'ry's voice again.

Thine to tell of youthful love;
    Thine the tale of younger days;
When the passions lawless rove;
    When our fancied bliss betrays.

But when wrinkled age appears,
    Wasting youth and beauty's bloom;
When the rolling lapse of years
    Clouds our mem'ries in the tomb,—

Little volume, then retain,
    In thy bosom's sacred trust,
Many a long-forgotten name,
    Whilst we're mouldering in the dust.

ADAM LAYS THE BLAME ON EVE.

FROM THE ITALIAN OF MENZONI.

When Jesus gave a groan of anguish,
>When he bowed his head and died,
All the mountains stooped and trembled;
>All the graves were open wide.

Then Adam, from his sleep of ages,
>Shook his hoary locks in fright;
And rising from the land of shadows,
>Looked with horror at the sight.

And as he gazed with grief and wonder,
    Uttered forth with sad remorse,
"Who's the one that's hanging yonder,
    Who's the victim on the cross?"

When he saw that 'twas the Master,
    All his soul was filled with woe;
And raising up his hands repentant,
    On his bosom gave a blow.

And turning then, with tears and weeping,
    To Eve he said with husky breath,
"You see 'tis for *your* sins and follies
    That He, the just one, suffers death."

ALL THINGS CHANGE.

The fairest blossom of the spring,
   Though beautiful and gay,
The gaudy insect's gilded wing,
   Must quickly pass away.

The star of beauty shines on high,
   Whilst, o'er the mountain's height,
It climbs the dusky-bosomed sky,
   Amid the lamps of night.

ALL THINGS CHANGE.

That star of beauty must decay,—
 Its course will soon be run;
The heavens and earth will pass away,
 When once their work is done.

There is a realm of endless day,
 Where love shall never end;
There is a life without decay,
 Where kindred souls shall blend.

There is a boundless space above;
 To loving souls 't is given,
To live a life of endless love,
 A life of endless heaven.

REMEMBERED JOYS.

Like earliest beams of opening day,
Unlocked by morning's saffron ray,
Chasing the gloom of night away,
    Remembered joys return to me.
E'en fancy's scenes before me shine,
Turning a thought to meet with thine;
In transports oft I call you mine,
    And seek no bliss but thee.

THE ORPHANS.

FROM THE SPANISH OF MELENDEZ.

When I, a tender youth,
   With young Dorila strayed,
We roved around the field,
   We walked along the glade.

With sweetest flow'rets oft,
   Her tender hand would twine
A garland for us both,
   And crown her head and mine.

Our childhood passed in joy,
  Each day brought new delight;
And every scene, and every hour,
  For us was gay and bright.

Our years of innocence
  Fled like the dewy morn;
And soon within our breasts
  Maturer thoughts were born.

And when I brought her blossoms,
  And laid them at her feet,
My heart, within my bosom,
  With throbs of transport beat.

With every glancing look,
  Dorila sweetly smiled;
And every prattling word
  My willing soul beguiled.

At length two cooing doves
   Displayed before our sight
The tenderest of caresses,
   The transports of delight.

Then like a passing shadow,
   Our childhood's days were gone;
And love with silken cords
   Had bound our souls in one.

THE POET'S FAME.

Before the miser's hoarded gold,
    Before the hero's name,
Give me the muse's sacred song;
    Give me the poet's fame.

Before a monarch's regal crown,
    Before a prelate's chair,
In nature's flowery lap I'll sit;
    The muse's wreath I'll wear.

Whilst demons strew the earth with blood,
    And savage wars arise,
The peaceful muse leads forth the soul
    To tread its native skies.

She loves to watch the starry hosts,
    Forever as they shine;
And all along their distant course,
    To trace the hand divine.

She loves the flowers that bloom
    Around the mountain's side;
She loves the creeping streamlets,
    That through the thickets glide.

OVER THE RIVER.

Over the river my loved one is waiting,
  Alone she is waiting for me;
But the river seems wider and deeper than ever,
  And the shore is too distant to see.

I sit in the darkness in doubt and despair;
  I await the approaches of day;
Whilst the dawnings of hope kindle slow in my
    breast,
  And the specters of doubt flee away.

The night and the storm-wind have passed from
    the sky;
The east is unfolding its light;
The mist on the water is passing away,
    And the shores now lift to my sight.

A mantle of beauty now rests on the earth,
    And lights up the stream with its charms;
In the transports of joy I rush o'er its waves,
    And my loved one is clasped in my arms.

OCTOBER.

FROM THE FRENCH OF COPPEE.

Before that the heavens in winter are veiled,
    Before that the streamlets shall close,
Let us list to the song of the last singing-bird;
    Let us look on the last blooming rose.

October still gives us a moment to gaze,
    Whilst nature's in glory arrayed;
Its mantle of purple, its forests of gold,
    Are beauties that wither and fade.

Such beautiful charms will not always endure;
  Yet in spite of the tempests that lower,
We may still have a moment to linger in hope:
  Let us seize on the fugitive hour.

Oh, then, let us build our last house in a land
  Where the skies are all bright and serene;
Where never the cold chills of winter are known,
  Where the fields and the forests are green.

MORN.

Soft the gold-encircled morn
   Lifts its radiant orb on high;
Swift the dew-bespangled lawn
   Lays its glittering splendors by.
The farmer seeks the distant mead;
The idler mounts his prancing steed;
But I'll away to yonder stream,
And gaze upon its banks of green.

There, beneath the cooling shade,
   Away from strife's alarms,

T' loiter on the flowery glade;

T' muse on gentle Delia's charms.

'T is there that nature's beauties shine;

'T is there I trace the hand divine;

'T is there to me 't is kindly given

To taste the loves and joys of heaven.

WHERE WAS GOD?

"In the beginning God created the heavens and the earth."
Before the "beginning," what? Where was God?"

Before that the heavens were in glory outspread;
    Before the stars and the sun;
In the boundless and far-distant regions of space,
    Oh! where was the Infinite One?

Before that the light, thin, nebulous mists
    To gather in space had begun;

Before that the bright beams of light had appeared,
>Oh! where was the Infinite One?

Before that the quick, kindling pulses of life
>Its mystical web had yet spun;

Before the first throbbings of love had awoke;
>Oh! where was the Infinite One?

Before that the dark, empty regions of night
>The cycles of death had outrun;

Before that the broodings of chaos had ceased;
>Oh! where was the Infinite One?

Eternal in God has the universe stood;
>Eternal the stars and the sun;

And the boundless regions of light and of space
>Are filled by the Infinite One.

Eternal in Him are the fountains of love;

Nor has aught, that exists, e'er begun;*

Eternal is life, eternal is love;

Eternal the Infinite One.

---

* Nullam rem e nilo gigni divinitus unquam. — *Lucretius de Natura Rerum.* B. 1, v. 150.

That nought from nought by power divine has risen. — *Dr. Good's Translation.*

Admit this truth, that *nought from nothing springs,* and all is clear. —*Ibidem.*

THE INDIANS.

By the banks of a stream on the mountain side,
Where swift o'er the rocks the bright waters glide,
Is a hillock of earth enveloped in shade,
Where the red warriors' bones in their blankets are laid.

There the song of the woodbird is heard in the spring;
There the young foxes bark and the cat-birds sing;

www.ingramcontent.com/pod-product-compliance
Lightning Source LLC
Chambersburg PA
CBHW032153160426
43197CB00008B/890